ANCIENT

Biswamit Dwibedy is the author of *Ozalid* and *Eirik's Ocean*. He has an MFA from Bard College, New York. In 2015, he edited a dossier of contemporary Indian poetry, translated from seven Indian languages, for the last issue of the seminal journal *Aufgabe*, published by Litmus Press. He is also a co-editor for the journal *1913* and the founder of Anew Print, an independent press devoted to translations from India. He teaches at the Srishti Institute of Art, Design, and Technology and splits his time between Bangalore, Mumbai, and Cuttack, Odisha.

ANCIENT GUEST

BISWAMIT DWIBEDY

HarperCollins *Publishers* India

First published in India in 2017 by
HarperCollins *Publishers* India

HarperCollins *Publishers* India, Cyber City, Building 10-A, Gurugram,
Haryana – 122002, India

P-ISBN: 978-93-5264-540-4
E-ISBN: 978-93-5264-546-6

2 4 6 8 10 9 7 5 3 1

Typeset in 10.5/13 Adobe Jenson Pro
by Jojy Philip, New Delhi

Printed and bound at
Repro India Ltd.

*

HarperCollins *Publishers*, Macken House, 39/40 Mayor Street Upper,
Dublin 1, D01 C9W8, Ireland

In memory of my mother

Annapurna Dwibedy

(1955-2015)

Introduction

Describe a writing that is part water, part milk, part rain.

Biswamit Dwibedy's *Ancient Guest* is a wet home for this description. I admire, intensely, the way in which parts of language substitute for parietal contact, or innermost touch, in this extraordinary collection. 'The sentence you never have flashes before your eyes,' writes Dwibedy, bringing our attention, acutely, to the instant in which something both arrives and is dispelled. The book attunes the reader to this exchange as it moves through themes of intense, erotic attachment ('Burn me something else'), and the relation to place as 'foreign' yet built, insistently and evocatively, through relation ('Friends become landscapes'). I was particularly moved by Dwibedy's governing interest in the image as something that disperses in the act of looking or observing: what 'had let the scenery disperse in their eyes'. In working so closely with the particulate matter of visible and invisible outlines, realms, bodies and even thought, Dwibedy convenes the book as a space that is working through or installing an idea about embodiment, even as it situates itself at the limit of sensation, the part of life and writing just before a feeling floods in. 'The voice opens to the body,' he writes, 'but the body cannot keep the voice.' The result for me was a kind of ecstatic ache in the tendons of my own heart at the end of reading.

This is a book to be read on a balcony, at midnight, or dawn, or dusk, when the light is between and nothing is understood, not yet, not ever. A world, or pre-world, is glimpsed nevertheless and deeply known in ways that aren't easily transmitted in language. Something flares at the edge of the book: 'A line that appeared when a spark fell.' I feel like it's my job to cup this spark and bring it here, into this sentence, so that you can see it in turn! I am honoured to write in support of this beautiful writer, who has written such a lovely and strange and very real book. I hope you find your way to the balcony of your own life, with these remarkable poems.

—Bhanu Kapil

Contents

GUEST

                            The year is
                                 soon to be our
                       innocent centre of
                                           what spans
                            eras   see him
                            get into
                            a blue
                                      twilight in

              a city spread like the news
              gusts from an afternoon—
                   an inward museum
                                 held by the
              birch and beech and elm

                       the 3 of us +
    a stone drinking milk
                       written on secret
         river unfurling

                         your hand on the edge
    under the table
         accidental touches
              recreating a scenario

    experiments re: the infinite
  productivity of language
    brittle oral tradition
               over adjacent states

in foreign accents

is a strand of the shore
       which means
   to witness a noise

was never found
   and is thus alive
& will go on giving

Alone

because it captures
a million colours as only
you can see

ancient children

they glow in the dark
they tease each other
with a nautical legend.

It is said
when the ghost of an asp
is covered in ash it turns
into three red birds.

One pleasures in the story of
people who spread
a mastery over the moon.

Another fled in return
independent of the compass
to sing & even out the sea

& powerful as many men
a woman of striking wind.

Sleep-state

Elsewhere all his life in
a city arranged on a violin.

I dreamt I couldn't regulate the crowds
coming in for eggs and coffee

sleep weighs down on us like mercury.

Inviting my body into folds of an apron

I go out walking to find the green
emits along their habit of
educating the eye.

Young stars I would like to paint
you confront, walking away from
the other side of the glass
seeing
also a non-entrance
a colour within it
this morning
that lasts forever

and have a good time! A good time!

Masks

Two rooms in different parts of the city that look exactly alike
with no intention of a secret communication between
the ancient objects that house them.

From there you can see the skyline, approaching weather.
    The cinematic
snow of the word *we* once said in the singular.

And letting me show you, if you are sleeping next to me, my
    peacock mask.

We do not expect any information, but a part of the chat had
    survived
as memorabilia—family photographs,

of people who have lost the same thing driving down that road.

And I tell him so every day. I tell him,
it's not my name until I act out what it means.

The sentence you never have flashes before your eyes.

He thinks you could conjure up the rain.
Someone should warn him, I act out
my falling as some bizarre optical illusion.

A possible hue it could have been
if I hadn't looked back

P(i)lot

I was beginning to feel like
I was
    the truth was
he had called it 'a night'
for no reason   a field
an isolation upon which

like an heirloom; eyes
rising up to meet—

the sky was concord.

Face against which forms the foreign
painting reportedly
an imprint on the silt.

Distance placed in bones

objects placed in language
to suggest spectrums.

On the surface of another river
one that exists along but never
the coast.
Can't be contained in itself
The outside I can't enter.

With the smile of an amnesiac
who doesn't remember the heat

Alarm

uncharted and windy
enjoyment without margin
understood through disappointment
impressed to the morning air

my stanzaic water
turns on all sorts of
ulterior motives

exchanged for a lapse
in proximity

cold head buried in cooking
provisional limbs
trim the wick
the flame
crushed, corroding
intimacy

A.M.

walking in
    —is
the noon today
 a delay between
arrivals
& will not look
you in the eye
will not touch
the skin
a con—

'fine' meant
in which
you can't tell
a fin
from the net
can't tell
what they want
from their order

Arthur

Our net of closeness and distance
'in a ball of yarn' or fabric of
fold by fold that unravels Arthur
singing—your understanding

it was a way of saying I want you
also to have the same experience.

A lens through which we look at
touch where his lips had listed
possibilities awaiting at the door

you wouldn't have recognized
or even know that I was there

Rustle

always at hand yet impossible to touch
phrases that match the moment perfectly

continuity of the melodic line as a back
ground emotion with twice the air

indulgent as a husband but not
faithful distance
voice didn't fade into

a response to particulars was
a rock carved
desire accumulating delays
between weather & refusal to speak
when he rudely shouts out what he wants
& my life is not a personal thing.

I think of us as friends
but not so early in the morning

eggs

Today's hunger used me like
instrumental syrup
a dozen eggs
strapped to your waist
the food was on
difficultly
difficulty
cultivated around us
smoke that
breaks this
inconsistent shade
invites
flotsam from a myth
a movie—thinking
winter would melt
under
'heat of moment'

Heat

Back in the heat of the kitchen
our usual
arousals casually explained
a rush: when people come in
how he crudely 'forms a fin;
a whole school' in the flipped
mirror of your eyes
moss made to look like a river
in wanderlust.

Can shimmer like
a sheen caught in the wind
craving a landscape

splayed under the sun

says something to himself?
Something else to the stove
I imagine you touching
depths in which
the sky doubles

Dear Sam

Attraction rubs off.
                                        You are
constantly touching the one I love.

Touches characteristic of a manuscript
 but not touches that indicate an author.

In an ancient book I read the body is considered
a meeting place of all the touches.

I depend on accidents while often touching
my own lips. These accidents I use
as a rule of thumb: whence and how they came

to be pleased and to please. My flesh beating
times suddenly still; confusions
the body can't remember; knowing that is simply
transitions on the screen

I said I but what I mean is my daughter, writer
sits and floats—'love is the grand use
one person rips off another'—

between songs
and dull parts of the afternoon

would be seen coming out of his house.

Body

(for Rosmarie Waldrop)

The voice opens to the body
but the body cannot keep the voice

I thought it were otherwise

my hopes were crushed by this knowledge.

Outside, a crowd unbuttoned
                    into exclamations
                                        exposed himself
                        glittering
                on a spider-web—

'all this is in the present
& in the mirror, every night

possibilities predicting
a tongue caught in
grain of sentences

I had badly wanted a story of my own.
Not a body but a form
without boundary or edge

Voice

contained in the trivial
something ancient, with no intention
a voice can cling to you
in the middle of a sentence
& pacing back and forth
your window, weather
acknowledged as an accomplice.

Their eyes had seen differently
creating a path now
for the moon just beginning to come up in
these books I have called my home
& morning somewhere else

I hear his voice takes
where a wing would form

In another myth
he'd have swallowed the sun.

His horoscope said it would taste like
any other fruit, when I thought
it was more like an egg
he was about to crack.

Rush

Our acts are mistakes
but nobody tells you
regulars regulate joy
in what one does
thrive in the lack of

touching repeatedly
calls out my name
or curse I mishear
the noise drenched
already in someone
else's attention.

A stir
under the rush
an eye on each
finger's spiral

hands on fire—
crowds collecting
clouds the colour of

sweat—
screaming
I love my job!

Fur

Your eggs are lovely, Hubble

unfurling at what speed are
moving away from one another

He knows good food arouses & inspires
& anything sung is always in the present tense.

Driving by, we saw signs of ruined nations
& dreams in which you resembled an animal
that had found extreme comfort in the plush hide

Carnage of my collaborative seductions

noon again
o blinding
lane/law/n

America is unreal
a sound you ride on
turning the air green.

And gather, hidden, on a window: a grassy gown:
this notion of a home you would have laughed at.

Swollen red river moves along the corner of
strike and it's electricity

incapable geometry.

An airy place unique to each artery
—this is that. This was that
which emits at night. Clear as vodka &
oiling down the wind with your two names.

To the coming together of their meaning in a sentence
are a river falling over. Incomprehensible men
will crush it up in a rage

and tie to his wrist
bones floating in the sound

I said the road destroys me
but going away I will take an inventory

Skin

what wills unfold
gilded on a glacier

in utterances common and untrue
the news is a déjà vu

glass orchestrating a long division

I saw him get into a blue van

I think the eyes are a museum

of salt drying on lashes as he slept
& I serve underneath when he
sails in & wets his beak in my
stream of
lover of

'single men and their single meals'

cheering the team into an embrace
abridged into a single week's
reversal of my desire for
another skin growing on
this morning
it's a mistake he says
that holds the bridges together.

And if you remember it extends
through watery flowers of unique self
cutting into borders

a scene in which our city is flooded

& I leave you with your many friends

Screen

I believe this is something you said:
'hopelessly confused by time'.

We watch a crack become a spun thing
as a forest begins to stroke the sky.

And as a separate form of cinema
we cannot quibble with the screen

within the face, the many faceted
raising an ocean you haven't heard of.

I thought the many strands were an accomplice
organized as a mosaic.

The problem is the end of
love & biology, an alliance, a single
mote of our encounter

like glass gave an insight

but nothing caught a reflection.

Seen

Benign night had led to a foreign place

had let the scenery disperse in their eyes
as constellations I read forth.

            'Burn me something else'
he said (and) I was afraid
of the moon becoming a laughing matter

the horoscope, a script I used to align
his experience to mine.

But he would not have understood.

He went on explaining instead an incidental light

a line that appeared when a spark fell

documenting the details of our conversation

Scene

Through the thin fabric I could see
the skin's becoming miles
away from your cheek—

was only a trick on the eye

friends become landscapes +

was nodding off at a bar when
I begged him to recognize

what one calls fictionalizing

who went to console the inconsolable sisters,

conversations one must apologize for in writing

we've declined the surprise by filling in the gaps

At the movie

I thought if I could project memories onto the screen
it would help me retain an image in my mind later, colour
accumulating, sculptural

—as a corollary, a group of neurons form
a miniature world—mouths facing each other
whose firing breaks a chain.

The many separate photons of a laser beam are so entangled
that it is as if there is just one photon in the beam—
but to see one has moved, there must be activity somewhere
symbolizing a change of particulars

—a room in which you could hear 'consciousness' at work—

if everything in nature is an inherent 'consciousness-ability', then
human beings have access to information about weather
    whenever

Borders

snowflakes streak the vast while
I am against you
like a skyline
& found what moves patterns empathetic viewpoints

established in repeating

a surface that curves smoothly to partly occlude itself

on the borders—on-screen as in any cell of an eye

—emerging from an ocean—

can organize a state-space—a space of all possibilities

in network activation

—maps—the colour of dusk—

—rush of smoothness—assuming—

if a surface is smooth
so is the image producing it

After Noon

light of recognition
reflected aimlessly
his body along
will hover.

As now you will
say: Can I?
Repeating
Let Me. Be Mine.
And the Many
in the forest turn concrete. Your breath
a staggering plateau. The delicate marriage
of bones.

An oar unravelled
whatever rippled
roughly shaped like
another orbit

similarities we must reclaim.

An I on the other side
the other hand, awakens
architecture. Like mica
inside the eyes.
Wheat, dirt
elongated seasons.

That move, so assured.

The sky multiplied within each vein. Your tender body in a blur. Now snow. Like glaciers in motion. To say, it's gravitational. Or subterranean heart will unwind the sea. To say: a brother, unformed, lives on, in green underwater of my home. Of stones. In neat pieces come undone.

Telegram

An architecture elongated along each vein now turns
delicate forest inside your body turns speechless and
unrecognizable which is beautiful and autonomous
like a sun spun of white threads and slivered
weather you can touch, taste, and it
moves you'll note   through the night   to your
wrist   in lighted vaults

a glass face and my pulse, chaotic, telegrams
escaping orbits: distant friend; bird, now tongue
inside fire, folded, it is summer, it is a flying I
watched you curve so gracefully
into your name
of impenetrable water
will not be photographed
will calmly drown

HUBBLE

__and the city

Walking creates a frame—
one pause modelled after another
till it is a bridge over the river
that cuts across your body.

Light crossing the water
replaced the leaves

some film found there
as events existing

vein after vein, grids
of information
scratched out
the eyes

The perceived sizes of the moon in its move last night
        were taken as evidence of the bird's flight
                        owing to their likeness to one another
                    they break into two small arcs

        on the surface of the moon, it's two small scars
eyeing an imaginary satellite.

                                He said, 'saved by the book'
but what he reads are inaccurate visual information
                            we have settled for.

A novel of thank you   not to be told at all
and certainly not as well told. Not as well told.

❁

I want to hear him through the night. The skin in its noon at night,
how there are many moons. But they don't melt into a bank
        because
glaciers rooted in the planet can become flotillas along our world,
        but not in it.

It might have begun as a vague sense of a distance, but it's
        luminous
by the time you arrive   white trim on a wave

what city isn't in conflict?

❁

The background, a feat of balance, a bone broken into wings

a shaky signature etched into the camera.

The distorted nudity he slips on

a recognition
grooved by your hand

a payment not an exchange.

A rejection of the visual idea to execute an intellectual one.

I'm still married, says the Bachelor.

His hardness released as a hinge.

Barter

Or perhaps two modes of thinking have crossed, creating
        the potential for an event
sentences are miniatures in which situations are contained

a kiss you never felt was the salt of my mouth

                                                            is how she kept track
                                                            of music inside a lark
                                                            in reference to

                                                leaves with eyes
                                                anticipating
                                                an accidental photograph.

A loaf of rain above my farm is an enormous ash, sheaf
based on what happened   over and over
an experience or emotion so aptly called your name

Plover

This doesn't correspond to something in the outside world
but
sifting through facts and things looking back
at you
roams a dialogue
between two discords.

As if such strokes were only missing. A hand that can
make this a face abandoned under the skin
& travelling in numerous directions
forms a ring
arranged as a profile
can be heard
by speaking into the old ruin

which is alive somewhere else as the basis of such doubling

as news stifled by the ones who wait

but with the tide, new patterns would unfold

characteristics of the shore dependent entirely on the plover

Film

Quotes, others, mine, times in which
I use them to describe what no one saw

as they often seem hidden by a web
        where the ideal is parallel

I would have drawn you accurately.

I was only writing to keep up with regulars
that regulate joy in poems I recognize
bewilderment and astonishment were sisters
as they read each other's work

Bream

As a boy, even before he knew how to read,
he wrote a book that would turn you blind.

I dreamt we were a part of his message,
the reading of a bream he touched

which no sheaf could recollect

weeds and stones the water employed
before evening turns into a sequence,
a riverbed

which at minimal intensity is a single pulse

becomes dust   of your absence

I love the letters m & o, the r laid into a vacancy.

Now we steal quotations and pad out poems.

If it is desire turning the timing of an event into a series
of delays
then isn't desire for an event also the desire of a delay?

quiet water
milked into
a grammar

as if maps
often pattern how moisture rising to the skin can process

the first map was of ephemera, streams

the surface was flawless till someone's seeing slit it

plagued by its course, it shrinks,

inside a grain of sand, a desire

to belong to the dead.
We are being read
by those who have no eyes. Gestures float

on your palms, patterns
the past follows
to protect us.

So why hide?

Bridge

Inventor of allusive shadows and promising letters,
out on your walk steps and stones are
states I call my present tending
the remainder we have termed syntax.

You cut my voice. Vein after vein—you turn to
ward your own body, a question mark, still

shrinking   a curve, a code
one step—and a foreign world appears

Operetta

Here buried an operetta
as our being together

brought out by chance

on a complicated dawn
chromatic values that enter
a room that is like a dream.

The first recognizable patterns
were fingerprints

difficulty of a foreign language
misplaced in a love for

impossibility, construe a film
and so we began to chart

the body rowed away in haste
a science of resisting sleep.

Assigning each star
to a new constellation

Carl

Our system of the great diffuse
could be used
as a metaphor on the sundial
but could never belong to any language

and since it is hard to deceive relationships between
limits of the sky and absolute brightness

Exemplary Midwestern charm
translated from   a strand
                                                   I weave
                                             to save thread
I must have misread: seashores
were the inspiration behind a science of speech

and a prominent American scientist believed
entire galaxies get caught in
a sense of intention in each silence
at the table
lost in a musical memory

Wick

Both particle and wave
the first spark is a stone
that burns to this day
with 108 names
& without a messenger
kept falling forth
of constant speed
with respect to all things that curve
are revered will
never come to an end

as a moon along its own earth
and everything we look at
is a lamp a map, recalled

as much sun as our distance from
decided upon a new home

relying heavily on a fertile wind

& as a part of a stellar arrangement

years of little movement
became a thin ring around the wick

Yolk

Growth rings surround the circumference of
            birch in snow
                    show
a strong climactic shifting

foreshadowed by letters   (seasons grow over our eyes)
                                     (and translating through the skies)

The first American to discover an expanding egg

based on unbelievable observational evidence

patterned in parts to correspond to reality

which echoed speculations about
the light that has been unable still
to find there's a future we will

proportional to our distance from one +
one equals the limits of my thought

said—secrets of the sky were essentially a photographic problem
they aren't phenomenon bound by their own appearance.

Honey

Not necessarily a continuation, but not a new beginning either,
his friends don't consider the messy details of neuroscience,
against the background of which the sentence
(what I'm supposed to say) is misunderstood.

Between the weather and length of all moonlight

whatever mistaken for the truth
just slightly beyond my reach

sound I marked for your arrival

that timely knowledge of no trace

but salt that lines these ships
mapped on a film of grease.

Golden shards floating
in the honeyed   I'd
leave it on the table and walk quietly back

To your instructional tonic
to the parched &
perched between position and stance.

Each stranger
is an assurance
that remains the news.

Hell

The body is evidence. Of patterns that entwine
and something invisible to our eyes can survive
our knowing a naming need not interfere
with what is between me and the delay to understand.

To continue as a sequence.
                                        I saw him involved in a strange sleep.
My staring at some parts of the film for a natural increase of
strands that change each scene.

They're in a new locale; singing in a language I don't
        understand.

It's a dream-sequence. Moving through the fog
in precisely choreographed steps

I sift through the scene till I see
crowds that refuse to share our love for a song
because to them, each step is effeminate; a shadow
of the presence we are too joyous to contradict.

And a wild fire caught under the influence
of improbable desires, as doting friends await

to connect empty glasses to their drinkers, who are too ecstatic
to remember white curtains swell anyways, oozing out of the seam
snow that covered the thin screen

and how I slip on the ice
is how the ringed horizon spiralizes in you: with disdain
for the classical design called proportions of the body.

Let me touch the axis.

Truth has no confines but a lower layer I'd strike
if the sun strikes the mirror in
which his friends broke
with his jokes.   In laughing
a person is bejewelled
breaking eggshells

Stay, see

I thought the leaves at this window of mine
were a bit of the sky wearing green
you tread to remember nervous patterns
but I've stopped saving the design

when the pollen floats
        I stopped in the middle of
                                if the lights are on
you have gone to bed
and will not wake up

                    (this on New Year's Eve)

names accrue a map of uses for the
                                    star-shaped
traced in flowers   beheld the world
                in closed eyes
                        a fissure thinking
        it's a vessel of
                        rice and wheat
spread out in all directions.

Measured in finest line-work
                        along his hands
never asked me for water
but clenched, a fruit
                and the world blurred
the distance between our homelands

The season's first prolific dust

now this ash all over your house

did you travel far enough?

Moving away from __ she said

'books are all we have left' of

those times don't correspond to

an inside but the very many stars

form a surface of __ under which

patterns rot +

the birds are drunk again

3 men alone at a bar

I want to steal
                    years abridged
into a wick   we are
always inside an enraged line

waiting

a pencil raised to the full moon.

But it wasn't you coming down
I caught
drying on his lashes as
they speak to me of my absence

the salt
a stain
on the seam
one should
contemplate the syllable.

Because I loved the mysterious
we lived on alms, misplaced &
what anybody else will not want.

We hear a mesh of wires, sensitive to touch
and colour of his shirt
arranged on a violin
becomes volume

A MYTH

Eirik the Red

Father of the first Finder of America
nurtured a vague little sense of religion.

He pleasured in when you cannot see
wanderings and intermissions
of violence and kindness

incoherent after finding grapes.

Prophetic North Star
Norse rose shape
glass hides honey, 'milk
weed I touch   floats'

linger luckless, but act like a voyage

uncertainty & importance of

drift of sand or snow

impossible to dress an unity.

Master's down in bed &
wearing Icelandic

read

One book says 'eider' and the other 'bird'

and said she likes how it sounds different each time.

Two versions derived from a red dress & his red beard

sought redress. Under a glacier named White Shift

two ghosts derived from the year 985 or 986. 25 set sail

count the 9 that didn't get married. A wealthy girl

deep-mined daughter of eastward brightness at night

drawing on information from within her own family

some fates remain as left out as described

        4 girls, 3 men, 2 birds and

one stone believed in unbelievable things lit up

inside the ice—a green compiled by his own son.

The Red

Diplomat and diarist notes,
Never had I seen people of such reddish colour
Dear Sir,
you are a name shared by every tongue

but nothing catches a reflection.

They painted clouds instead to depict
what friends tell you about your life
and you think is a prison. A prism

not a distinct direction the light scatters in

the waves come in from the inside.

It's a gorgeous view, she said

he's beautiful as an animal
trapped in the wind—
a girl
by the museum

for contemplation
each movement
a fold of that time

I thought the book was a war
in the middle
of which we
just run
out of lives

Reed

said I shouldn't name
  dead silent centuries
light on an insomnia
a sound I count on
each finger denies
  surface experience
I mine by
telling no one

burnt corners of
icebergs touching
 rake, reed, stem
changed hands __
two landscapes in
memory followed by
one voice without

White Shift

We have no map, he claimed
    according to the crystal sea
nothing turned green in one
version of the legend both
        of them promising young men
  but Eirik wouldn't give up his faith

raven and wolf are the
  impersonal in the age of the individual
      would have gone in or
at least a little closer

to the wind a chest
of gold children
with red hands

they're punished for having hidden
travellers counted into an ideal couple
who could scarcely recall having seen its like

Manuscript

and there sighted unknown lands

at the mercy of contrary winds

wild grapes are grown here as

a way of counting longitude

860 names ornament a part

of the world called undiscovered

gods go on wearing diamond

wind arrived at a historian's

ambition marked by removes

Year Unknown

Little Cousins—
    The weather is very cold here. We the students of the white
    throne have never seen anything like it.
We thought we were home but it is difficult to not be fictious in so
    far and fair a place. Sometimes a letter says
you will see me someday but what I send
is always badly aimed
and we miss that fine edge. We love the black buzz of the marrow
too homogeneously. Our sacred neighbours are angered by the noise
but still send their sympathy, insisting I live always drowning
the pronoun, a faded flower, the difference between a letter
and a poem: a little book in the grass. We go out walking and find
the green emits along their eyes & at this time
going against the appearance of lover. And leave my kisses,
a faint note in pencil. The wilderness about my breath,
Called Back—
The Dead need a boat to carry their grave wealth.
Make them know I love them, though our alliances
are losing foothold, and to trace them would be a huge burden.

glow in the dark helm of

awe on your arms I sa

id like it here can I

repeat enough times

just above your wings

encircling orbits adjust

history weighs warriors

Open

before turning lights on
the blue bodied boy
                god goes on colouring
does he know how to resist
                    each morning 2 summers
                    riddled we are seers of
a sail restless and his memory
just stops by your hand
reaching for the day's mysteries.

      Now it was time to think of coffee.
or syllables one must contemplate
when he calls out
a question you mishear
      though that is not what they want.
We don't call that frost but
kingdom proposed to other things

Movie

lengthening shadows and
sacred nights cultivate in
the vicinity of I don't know
how anyone could take the sun
in mouth the most aquatic
novel's main theme is renewal
why one body falls and another
doesn't see him perched in it *is*
silently coming down again

in the forest means a tribe
dwelling will reconstruct
lovely Hubble, Edwin
this memory seems strange
step by stone who gathered
the sea into mild tremors—
sky enclosed as if in a letter
    by your memory I have
known little of you

Bird Two

Stands on fringes of the stead and decides
to where new voyages might be
the warm, worn hand, a map
written on water and I thought
                    I saw
that glittering, a semblance.
An accident can look like you were trying.

There is someone here who trespasses
where I was. Or are you just
an aftertaste; a mistake the tongue could make.

Bits of a song, meanings from different names
spread into a purple called your body.

He knows each colour was conspiring to see
our hands forge a likeness. A paltry resonance
once called laughter. A storm caught inside a book
a pattern you cannot distinguish from the ropes and
ribbons it makes of your body.

Through the thin fabric I could see it doesn't mean a piece of cloth
but
secret and fictional I
proved unpopular and discarded.

Migration followed a similar pattern
a journey forever forward home that never was
pushed out by unfavourable weather
attracted to promise of new land
named after patron saints,
thought mind a mesh of unfolds
and within secret fictions
fractals.
He had red hands that often changed colour as we worked,

and everything touched turned an attribute
of the immaterial world

devoted to another man
as dear as own brother
so how to count
when he comes in
at unpredictable hours
incarnate in the animal
sacred endearment
some relic snatched and
then returned.

Carrying entire landscapes in one hand
and assuming the sun to be a ripe mango
body raised to orbit around pleasure
was the fee.

Captivating accent,
doesn't enter your mouth but flies across
a mild curse
under which a wave
is a drop of sweat in the ocean

someone else's experience of another winter, a horizon
made out of an eye in love with gravity, the snow
rolls in on waves and waits
there for centuries to sculpt the air
naming things that never returned.

A saint was wrongly alleged to believe
the body was beyond
lines each palm would unfold

trees align into a green that heals the eye
he carried in his pocket turned ice.

believed the next winter would be milder
            and moved further north
in search of two meanings of the word
defy their difference with the distance from
a home around your neck
wearing the season's new colour

Bird Three

both thunderbolt and diamond, my friends
gently helped by the sway of
spread along to other parts
symbolizing the union of compassion and
the dark and obscure
wringing his hands over a map of the world, thinking
the obvious analogy is with water,
& the earliest example of writings
found in ruined cities that line the now dead riverbed.

At the trace of a fingertip
the three strands from a thread

660 or 661

Dear Cousin

I bring you a Fern from my own Forest, where I play every day:
It is August 1876. She writes 'Loved and little Sister—
we call her the minute hand.' And when thought wavers,
it is certainly to test the sentence.

The same could not be said in Eirik's day.
He had a shorthanded sickle and an iron blade
shining in each hand
and even those were scarce. Eirik or his blacksmith
would heat up a finger, purify it further.

And draw at the mouth of the Swan, an island so fertile
you would have had to call it green.

The duck population is lower now.
Mother is timid for you, remembering
dark mystical tradition.
A community taken up by truth
excluded allure
of the noise in which
you trace specifics
of infinity, by itself
to infinity, by itself.

Ancient lake and trace unknown
a feather could follow you home—
a flake of snow, distinct and lost in

projecting the self into action
from barbarism to civilization.
A small short-lived settlement
promised growth

a saint with short bloody reigns
feels at images of an island

for all our mistakes
had actually started a landslide

'I'm burning'—the child said,
and nearby, on one hand, stood
that which betrayed our trust

Wander and return
grief for grief
pagan pages sailing in fleets
winged young boys glittering
over fields and fields of
now covered path
turned murderous

of where and when they met
connecting resources
distributing the news

men go roving over
the mouth of the river
whose shield is thunder

I look at you and a wonder
takes me weaving a fine mind.
The sea too close kin for our story
takes such strange turns.

Massacred children and forgetting queens.
The king is drinking with his diplomats
and scattered unmistakable characteristics
across whitecaps or nightcaps.

Dear Body, Bird,

A letter always feels to me like autumn
across the shape of your eyes
and in the centre of desire—a quotation.
Lovely alien floating in the throat.
A lily found there.
Passing from personas to portraits,
pleats presented in the throat
though I am to recollect
the arm reaching for.

Birds amend homewards in stern pleasure.
I wish they would tarry the frost
I wish the delay were kinder, a precious inn
painting years we shall journey when you come home again.
As a proof of recognition
the road is faithful. Vegetation continues along it
like yellow paper—the purest of all regions in the garment of life.

In tatters under the windless evidence
that stands at the heart of its mystery.

Its beauty relates to the silver
moon under down lids
and in the back of my throat
mechanisms that disappear into a language
I do not speak

and mourn that loss in a foreign tongue.

It's snowing here again. Green divided by white.
Thank the dear little storm calmly detaining me
between a remainder and as the brackets indicate,
a little world of sisters

recurrence of nomadic conditions

the water takes on a human voice
indeterminate directions it sparks
measured into paper cuts what is
the ancient to you Sir
of indifferent worlds

the submarine behaviour a sailor
sings to icicles around his beard

unpredictable weather
we've treated the dead like a king
or vice-versa

two versions of claiming ancestors
but we couldn't have measured
the distance within them doubling
now we go back to saving daylight

The past coming true at a staggering speed

returning free from snow
now the sun, a disaster
the year 1000 was one in
which they were not content
with fixed horizons

the fragrant grass
breathing in slopes when
centuries await ahead.

They've decided to winter there.
They've discussed amongst themselves
what country it might be

but before he could answer
they sighted a glacier

and everywhere birds
wherever there was water.

In a sea I put to sleep
whose hard home is knowledge
his for the taking, but he takes time.

Edwind

It is he who discovered the olive
not a replica on display
strangers caught saying you are the opposite of
the body wrongly affected by the mouth.

The light swerves out shirts and
my body grows to the left.

He sees it as a face
let me touch your lips. They are mine
no need to feel duped—it is a play

on the word
Body—a pause or delay
what word isn't
the name of a
seeking
I wear out

Islands

We see the sea reaching precisely
for the subject is a shipman's card

I suggest you write on it in red.

In the welcoming light the dead
have shed their skin & become
more than I see when what I cannot see is-
-lands to which you have lent your name.

Must have been a life more fully lived than
here add an I to his sons of unreturned
men sentenced to sea realized they were

farther inland. Some were driven back
and some explored the landscape there.

DEVOTEE

Scene One

The Master was incurable with Lily in his throat
as he listened to the line: *I want to hear you break your silence*
and let the echoes that bind peak to peak
remain incomplete
like gossamer: atlas of the unknown
on your chest   Chant: *'you've entered*
my soft-core & let each nerve
ricochet. A hymn
that you need
a hundred hands
one thousand eyes
to awaken
the missing vowel
mother of pearl
scattered into
another world
where water is useless
& each stone priceless

steeped
in the body
offering a flow.

The loved one's voice
remains perched

on the other side of sleep

forged out of chance

each pull of breath is
contours driven into the heart

that makes the hand now hover

across that sea he is
standing on the shore.

The water could not attract him anymore.

Scene Two

Master had been discoursing about the architecture of
each and every nerve, in which like lightning,
a mere pupil
swiftly got on after finishing his meal.

Reaching for the wretched life with dispassion—

when it enters our eyes it imparts its lines
to the night that never was.

Thinking of progression, both linear and orbital,
because of his friendship with a devotee

had been thinking of nothing but
snakes, birds, coyotes   moving away from
and into that kingdom of half-closed lids.

Nor is there benefit in opening the eyes completely.

You might be invisible to me
but I count on you as morning to
strand by weave.

(mango)

Soft directions
meet and mesh
a rock formation

will surpass any scripture.

The most primitive fruit
is the shape of a heart
gone hard.   Fossils follow

a ghost in the dirt.
                    A householder

who is a true devotee
lives in this kingdom of
tracing patterns.

Unparalleled study of
muscular activity.

Generating heat
but no waste.

Heightening visual acuity

are coloured oils
in the cones of the retina
swans & eagles use

or springs unattached
to the nectar of
whom do you say you return to,
with your eyes closed,
when no one else is awake?

Scene Three

A honey leached through the living.

A flood leads to remarkable fertility
in a cage
to protect the heart, a kind of glass
used for domestic purposes
remains engrossed with the reflection.

Most sensitive messages don't trigger a response.

Breaking the shell of glass, the reflection
begged the Master to keep him alive

as possible by the waves, the many colours

the Master makes his own, there are
different colours because it is contact with the

thousand petal really black Lotus   floats
sometimes Mine, sometimes not

Scene Four

The colour provides a continuous network
trapped in his name, the sea was
millions of messages crossing

'drama of the body.'

The obvious analogy is
with saying

this is that which has no colour of its own

and is true for all nights
but not the ones that follow.

And it thus follows that
in repeating the name you
get closer to the formless
way it acts

with your eyes closed may appear
without attributes and release
from the heat of currents dispersed

across great distances

a unified body

Scene Five

Drops of water
gather his name
on a red-hot frying pan.

The people realize
he looks out of the world
into the mouth of the unknown
& exclaims 'Ah!'

Gives up intimacy
to light the path of
a more pleasurable science

after pondering over the image
when his mind is on the wave
may just produce a mild sound
but leave no wake?

An ordinary fly
yearning for honey

calculating difference
between shade
and shadow

from the flowers

unattached
to vegetables

his companion
word 'alone',
'only'.
'nothing else' etc;

Scene Six

Smoke soils the wall at the temple, was
resting after his noon meal, in the afternoon, A

bout the sun in them the Encyclopedia says:

Smoke is the visible product that appears to be
emanating from breathe. But how else

does the body say 'I am Him'. This

'O Jamuna. If I have not eaten anything to-day, then
may your waters part so that we may all walk to the other

end of sorrow

and think that the self is dead.

Can a man be sure about that? We are fooled by the
combustion that is carried away by a current of gases and

resting after his noon meal. In the early afternoon, N.

Spider and its Web

In the early evening, had been discussing
regarding the sports in our arteries
& ejected in an excited state
a field of snow, in which playing,
sensations swirl and form that
unchangeable
act of kindness

emerge as
spiders that make many uses of silk glands +
don't throw away the unbroken black sky

which provides silk towards
the ease with
which
the spider moves over the field
causes to understand the infinite
through our limited mind.

That he is both instrument and matter.
One web,
the thread on which the young ballooning
spiders migrate
is both amazing and difficult to understand
but a closer look at the dark and you see
he is none other than
what dwell in the devotees
after touching the web.

Scene Seven

Even the Flood-tide and Ebb-tide
were not notes independent of the hours
to a young devotee, who then gently put forward the question:
what is the purpose of life?
considered in a newly learned sequence
in reference to the springs
of compassion,
    the Master said:
The fish feed off the stone without attachment
and told us that first know this detachment and then everything
    else
will come like Crabs in the Ganges during Rainy Season

And elsewhere, in the same book, the end of hair
divided into a hundred parts and then each part
is further divided into a hundred parts for
then alone you will not be able to differentiate
between your home and a foreign country.

Scene Eight

Used to give advice to his devotees
involving the use of the cyclic during such fickle weather
& implored the disciples
to live by themselves.

Said: the bees sit on flowers only &
though they like to live worldly lives, they see that
this universe is transitory, alone is Real and
in the secretions
is the Math & Mission

immaculate young boys

Their attitude is that of Ravana, that excellent pundit.
He does a great deal of farming.
Somewhere he is both worldly and alone,
enjoys both yoga and bhoga; the one of knowledge
and the other of you may wash a thousand times
the cup that the householders very often use,
but it is never clean of the taste as after
touching the lips of a true devotee.

Bubbles

The Master had been busy in discourse
or indirectly observe, bubbles on water
are as if planets, and so I
open the lid of the pot &
see the birds fly into the sky!
In our day to day life,
for example, if there is a fish,
it would let bubbles small and large
seen on the water surface &
in chlorophyll
sunrays very feeble nonetheless
was a flower
but it changed to a bird,
that is: it found
your helping hands
to be mine alone
in all my work and plays
not disappear
floating
into the separation between
orbits.

Master Alone

Feeding on the bread of stars, at footlights of the ardent lover
their relationship, now reduced to a metaphor, a cluster of
knowledge
that turns perception to the proof as one searches for it.

Units of measurement become frames to reveal the radiant serpent
ever-changing in the night sky.

This freedom is the result of that recognition.

'And so I descended from the sky and awakened you,'
said the bejewelled animal
to the simpler earth choked by muddy fragments.

And lines of landscapes appear choked when
expressions of the face cease to manifest

'two hands only intertwine by the extension of their shadows'

as the shape of the word 'anonymous'
because it is incomplete
a sequence turns to an extension
seen in the nature of blood.

And the frequency in question
is the proof allowed
to find no utterance.

Scene Nine

Gurgling sound when an empty pitcher is dipped
                    measures
how to live in this world. Marked
with the removed, the Master said, 'If the water
                    answers again'—
It turns into honey through his fingers
first sinuous,
then meandering, and then braided.

The land dragged behind with ample evidence
                    underneath the plume
that wandering curve of epochs & events
in constant movement. He left
        a new kind of wave
a discrete oscillation
      in that trade between
sculpting and
the occurrence in question.

Secrets

A beloved lay disciple
suffers from a weakness, who on Annapurna Puja
came to see—What is the seed that makes the rocks
respond to this weather? That must be a creature
of habit. The rock comes undone,
peel by peel. The water soaked
soils move downslope to a gradual
accumulation of snow.
Glaciers grow. They radiate outwards

like a crowd on the edge of a burning field
or how a drop can cause a wake. On which
He still rakes the scene for a sign of his friend.

We picture facts to ourselves
in numbers that manifest
the science of the endless.

The Master said, 'One's mind undergoes change
like Rahasya about the young devotee

if lust and anger injure a man he must stand the epidemic doubled
and continue to rise.

In the marrow, something concentric.
The consequence evolved in the form of the body,
as a certain confusion, corresponding to distinguishable parts.

His shadow falls on this thing and that and they become attached

or will. When He says 'Yea', everything comes to pass and
when He says 'Nay' everything comes to a standstill.

Hammer
and manliness. It constantly being struck by the hammer.
Let's begin our analysis of pressures. That meals
should be, that food should be, per day at the regular times
was the crest-gem of the doctrine.
Indicates what did not deviate the rishis.
According to your misfortune you would be able
to endure anything. He was whistling
as he walked along. The Master sang, as if to himself.
The world is like a sea. And living amongst the
wild animals, craving for the shore does not depart.
This is called surrender and unless one has this
there is no escape.

Secretes

A few other devotees came to see and pay respectful homage to the Master, whose teachings were by then unagreeable with authorities. He came from a noble family noted for its piety and other spiritual qualities. One of his remote ancestors was an intimate companion of

and thus the blood of a great lover (of God) flowed in his veins. A love that had been merely waiting to manifest itself in all its sweetness

and irresistibly attracted by the intoxicated path.

I thought it must have been my way to the prime grove, but what can I do, I am lost! I looked to see what the matter was and I found that a water-snake had seized the bullfrog. The snake was an unripe teacher, who had to go through this agony because his love had no poison. The bullfrog's defence mechanism, however, is instinctive. The teeth of the snake are curved inwards.

One touch can cast a spell.

The bullfrog's lungs might deflate after death, but he's really trying to draw a map of this swamp with the edges of his breath. And as a result the snake suffers too. And speaking of food, the devotees devoured his words. The Master was now speaking in such a beautiful voice

Not lecturing for lecture's sake but talking about his realization. Everyone says whoever goes to him does not return to the world. Living in the world may have a little blemish, but this does not bother Him, floating in the water, a tasty morsel

He shares with the others.

Scene Ten

What's seen

is a screen

and messages don't seem to cross the threshold

but go back to hope

the reaching for an infinity that began at the navel. Along the spine are six lotuses. They open inwards. And in that light you couldn't tell if he had his veneer swathed or had instead withdrawn, like light inside a lantern through which we see this image of the fourth plane with twelve petals & the fifth plane with sixteen petals which eases the great pain in anyone. Then comes the lotus with two petals.

You may think you have touched the light but in reality you cannot because of the barrier of the glass. It should reflect our unwavering thoughts. The glass covering the lantern is the obstacle making it so. This again lies in the mind. Like sentences not yet produced. With each utterance forward the space of knowledge changes its contours, until it becomes a swarm washing over the queer edges of whose body becomes the message itself.

Scene Eleven

It was Sunday morning, April 8, 1883. The Master looking like a boy was seated in his room at shrine

Swar. And near him was another boy.

And several other devotees gathered by and by. Replied, 'Friend, you have painted your eyes with the dissonant zeal for that state of other passions. Many lay people even know the minute details of a frog.'

The Master said: 'The poison of the frog's head gets absorbed around the eyes, causing them to grow dark and beautiful.' But this was only possible in Bengal, and only back then, owing to the biology of those times. He also believed there was something in the air that night that makes you forget the world. Chaitanya deva had this piece of wood from the sacred grove   & the ocean floor moved to the glories of the dark longing you see in an aspirant on the path of devotion. Often used to bring the inner organs into control. You breathe in one image and breathe out a different night

for this is how sensual pleasures appear more and more tasteless as love grows   & consequently this shrine of the body; it has no need for so many lights   just illuminate it with the lamp of wisdom. It is the maya that deludes.

'The mind soaked in worldliness is such a damp match stick.'

Worldly people are like silkworms under the control of the cocoon.

So how must one light the lamp of knowledge in one's heart?

It is said in a song: '*The landscape will tell you what to do.*'

Gopala

'Burning camphor and wood, I wanted to fly off to the other side
and return   recounting experiences of an illusory world
                                        what happens when you burn camphor,
            nothing remains.' I wanted to fly into, a new form of
coincidence

when wood is burnt at least a little ash is left. But the formless
    Master Mahasaya is a salt doll.

Enters the ocean to measure its depth and emerged dressed in
    pearls.

Each one counting the name and glories of keeps his mind fixed
on the hums and hunches, will not be able to tell
one instance of bhakti from another
unfounded in the substance of flesh, and
shell, and seeds

nothing remains after we concentrate our ideas about wood.
'Wood is our selves to a higher plane.

if this is not so, why then the scripture, which could have been written on the colourless, of no tomorrows   placeless or colourful tomorrows which is a new use of the body?'

And you should say: *Only his voices are* a Permanent Substance; all else is illusory and roam & room and sat by M's side.   Master asked him, 'Why live up to two hundred or two hundred fifty years.

When what is probably the original word is also the corruption inside

no force on earth could make them out

but their aim was to attain the instance of camphor. To disappear, after an instance which cannot be realized, which cannot differentiate between 'green' or unripe.

He said: 'He is always in and out with the Lord.
Not the Lord of the Universe but my Gopala!

Scene Thirteen

Was discoursing against random & impure ingredients. Said
pearls, diamonds, tattoos on the flesh must be kept pure
of impurities which multiply, from one to ten at night
we are all seated in the panchavati, then
how does he dare make a remark like that?

He wanted to discourse on a particular kind of blindness
but some of their friends do not like this.
The Master sang: Of water,
Furthermore from the escaping deposits
    at the basins

a soft math
                                        to office.
                        Such foliage
then why do I eat the fruit you offer me?

    and drink the taste of
                                    I love
I do not know, friend. Perhaps the smell of flowers
or the red colour of molasses that does not disappear
is also a kind of work. As you develop, your world,
time of day, to his nape, the surface of these waves
take refuge only in a slope inside the Earth.

Swan taking the milk

speaking to Devotees who stood close
realized were putting the lilac in the mind
though nothing stays inside one's mind by
artificial means.

    'Like the swan are those
who think they prey on the river till it turns
to sand

    and then they be like ants

and take the sugar.'

Again, the world is a mixture of milk and water,
at night there are equations that capture bliss to
a physics spreading over every word is near and
dear to me is Everywhere deepening the sweetness
made possible by widespread use of sugar

Vesper

Let us pray to bestow on us the unwavering

probability of recurrence.

    The moon has no colour of its own

this is the highest stage of bhakti. You cannot say:

  Transparent the wind has no colour and hence it cannot be

    You did not touch me nor have I touched you.

        You are pure as fire

      but would make fire look as if

  having itself been melted out

    there is much more to it than Night, pray

he will have the same thought in this hour of separation

since the five elements are at work, as

long as he doesn't know he is the body

engulfed in extreme tranquil passion

(Intoxication of the opium)

It was on a Sunday in spring (March), few days after Sri 's words, affectionate tones, serene-look and his devotees looked around him with wonder and

efficacious as opium, said 'Yes,

He's in the room.' M: 'How long has he lived here?'

Was talking with them and smiling. No sooner had

he been unable to banish the thought of Sri that he

was talking with them M entered the room

and said to the boys.

All joined in the laughter.

And took a seat.

Folded hands, like one

o'clock in the afternoon and it came to that his second function seems to have been to stand by his sleeping revolutionized the facts about opium and its various use produces euphoria, relieves anxiety, makes one feel

the day he learnt his laughter

fed a peacock.

And his own body answered back

curtain of feathers

prevent his being awakened by noise.

__________ told the Master once that ____________

said 'There! He has come again.' Having seen

suddenly I have seen him before that but the very sight of him

disclosing to him in __________'s first few visits about

his relation with the newly arrived devotees. Devotees who would

later renounce the world and live the book that the Master asked M.

to come again.'

why he used to come even when not spoken to or asked to

Scene Sixteen

discussing about the Lord in the house of the Master said,
follow the path of the states and the
reflection: that alone is substance
and causal bodies are only
the knowledge of
the soul within
that state of identification

'I am He' 'I am
the path of bhakti. A man cannot easily get rid of
the 'slopes of know
no edge'

the water
tasted divine
He accepts that a rift may consist of multiple faults
He said
one cannot simply explain away the states
all these gunas-sattwa, rajas, their kingdoms
have always been a living thing.

Landscapes reveal an embodiment of
practices they say the truth should never let
the devotees of
Oneness,
Disregard the horizon

as barriers. He does not
regard himself
as Himself
in a Wax Garden, beneath everything glowing
you may see
a wick
blind

Mirrors

Impulses on the other side of this afternoon cause
a pause or delay. The air turns to water as
the weather turns to colour
and desire turns to a stone whose
edge turns to an abyss as
you turn to an impulse
causing breathlessness.

What good hands to come undone in
and come undone they do—all the elements
against the glass pattern

whatever that shimmered
breaking the reflection.

❁

It's a conversion, they say
                                        a translation of a quiet phase
that keeps repeating itself, only in different cells
in different bodies, distributed, equally along
folds of the skin that secrete, fade
more smoke than smell.
More colour than air.
Not weather anymore but a sameness we felt as a pleasure once

and thus the importance of hardly any contact.

The question itself interfered with both memory and fact.
The audience though had been warned about such a reaction.
Had been asked to not necessarily recognize memory as a fact.
Now recent results indicate that abstraction offers a salvation.
The painter confronts it most directly, in the kind of image
whose meaning would come to you without your thinking.
As a result of signals to the muscles, yet only in part
because your body responds to the surrounding.

Sometimes this procedure will not shoulder the difference

at the price of a hundred years, some intimate delight
        as an overtone, at the fringe
of the stream, certain feelings are felt, known, as states so clear,
They allow neither image nor reflection.
The molecules, 'unconscious' data, because
To their eyes, the word 'me' or 'I'
deserves no individual. Should be regarded as primitive
sleep the moment you cease to be mere survival—
Dear breath, the unknowable phenomenon
is repeating within the both of us.

ERODE

Sparkles

Stay there on screen,
admiring data pull
from some satellite string.

Trace a curving shore to summer
each morning

can occur in any month, mouth. Notes
on silence and distance at work
odd correspondence
you cannot count on vows.

To perceive is to touch a crack
unaided the eye each morning

to horizon
undocumented letters
faltered conversations
echo bejewelled
no map
to guide the fault through
this imposing earth.

Erode

The horizon fractures
            the eye into events.

Streams of water during a heat wave
like mica sparkle against the black ground.

Quartz, grains of sand
consist largely of ancient rocks,
a watery fruit

weathering the bulk of what moves freely
amongst crystal structures

as milk we thought he was drinking.

Emit

an ash

into the air,

causing a stir among the believers

who'd been waiting for proof
that he listens to you
and was thus alive,
or will forever live,
like any other stone.

Shale

Dip seaward
    spill
into a mosaic

on the cross-vein
seam

of sun stone

upward flourish
of an undercroft

effects of the wake
reveal no oar but
a pattern beneath

vortex in the eye prevails
deepening the green easterlies

steered by adjacent fires
an electronic river

restarts

Thunderbolt

The prolonged rain
on a sloping curve
is the vehicle
that incarnates as
slow drifting story.
Whereas the white horse it
hunts is an individual
unable to make up its mind. Acting often, on opposite effect, a
weird wind
between a horse running wild and the rain is a bolt trapped
or otherwise how I'll be able to trace
shallow seas dare not disturb.

When you are asleep my skin absorbs the sun
retains a certain landscape. The way it melts is the opposite
of how you
open your eyes in the morning unable to differentiate between
the warm presence from this ice age
made possible by a single event.

Satellite

each name thinly about voices connect
continents
perched by the water
the life it will take
to another movie
moving (in
across the skies your hand)
if you close your eyes who died
when no one cried were
this time a coincidence
as if the screen could not withstand
unseen still blinded
by our disbelief.

piple, shiprock

Carved a pattern
with the calibre
of a geometry.

An echo unreturned
twice the days
it rained on an address
arrived at
wrapped in letters
like weather ricochets

patterns on paper that
guide our conversations

to the road you drive through
in your sleep of
116 nights
dressed in the fall
a birthmark
to become
the best example of
abyssal histories.

Hesychast

Cosmic imbalance manifests as
riots over cities still warm
from hands that open a door

spreading the light shock

a remnant

pauses all over the sentence

as a gift misplaced
in the meaninglessness
of pleasure
                                        lingers
traces

couldn't communicate the news
because the clutter would
muddle the meaning
said the horoscope to the day

look closer:
                constellations swirl in the
sweetness of his spit
oceans roar in
the salt of his sweat we're
breathless without his words

Can only tell the story in reverse
to create a future without memory
who went in to the closet to pray
& left   a bell ringing

for spiritual awakening
over a bevy of boys
in an elliptical path

their fingers
begin to look like yours.

Or like a landscape you used to visit
as a child each time you draw
strengthening the past

caught in a film of dust

and thus related to the underpass
over which, his body's movement, a rhythmic action
can only be described using a handful of drawings.

Alive between two pauses
things that determine the length of my stride

a balance from which evolve
elaborate wings.

Over an infinite number of relics.

He didn't move,
he rippled. He said
even his muscles had muscles
that had been smoothed out
and only the seams of the gown were
exposed to the air—

Not seen as a continuous thing
but resistance over which
the body stays afloat
                    a tangent where the entire edge moves so
                                                            freely it becomes

corner of an eye
an open window
and foil
invisible views
where young monks set themselves on fire.

Moniker

Where each silence suggests
        new states of being together,
the difference between desires
to carry
on a sort of conversation
that has no name

under the spread of the impersonal.

Would have disappeared upon naming

putting together seasons
                                        to unfix the golden underside,
                        a group of muscles
in the engraver's eye

is beaten into the shape of a thin gold leaf
                        set to destroy the fine weather of a picnic.

On one side of the sheaf, shadow
                        and on the other, connected to the sheath

was the Sun himself

breaking through veins

heaves a path
                            of subdued interests.

Most probable uncertainty
            emitting this atmosphere

looks for an instrument of passage
        in in morse completeness

decorative homophones

babble

a new form of politeness.

❁

Parks

to enact for a moment

the abrupt goodbye.

And the coast is a single line frayed by the noise
        from which conversations come as a gift

and cities bear fruit like weather hangs
      like bridges across distance magnified by the
                                                                          moon
brighter than it has been in decades.

Catching at the bow of the vessel

shed some skin or become

a rock's modus operandi
                an overlap
uphold

filthy and forgotten jewels.

Compete in moving with the slender snake

in a glance between two photographs

so many of you I already do not know

like unnamed constellations
        existing as energies within the body.

Or like three strands of the stream pleases

the child of three roads who   renounced attraction for
      worthy cruising

urging me to cook up for someone else
                His love for his lover's whip.

The young man's hair rushes out of the village
        signifying a withdrawal from the visible world.

                His hips naked in the cold sea are
absent in any mode of making love.

He covets the pleasure in the lotus, its hundred petals, a place in
        the night
where the object exists without being identified

and *ratna* never means jewel in the RV
                    though the lotus or the thunderstorm on the other hand
                                        show the conversion

of sound to sight that would seek
                                what sort of ideal mate buzzing like bees

chant

& the reluctant glass withdrew

a reflection

                                    in return

                                                            is an insight

                                                                            into the mysterious

Each note hung on the web
of a sentence largely imagined.

The child holds the camera
in a series of photographs
that feign togetherness

in which the colours erase a distance
famous for all it holds together
like a soft voice over the telephone
deciding in a haste to give
the event asked of the sanctioned body

emitting such frequencies as habit
works from within
and cannot be named until

repeated enough times each day.

11.11.11

Deposits of clay flow into the green
that will marry an inlet
to the underlying symmetry

a path
the prism reflects

arc, belts,
cyclones cross the entire expanse
connected as fireworks, volcanoes erupt
and monks meditate on the same thing

eating nothing but that grows in hiding

a curve
the swans follow
dressed in their finery &
interrupting the flow that day
was the water.

Bright along the edge of the ocean
we have now designed a light
which won't fall apart in our hands.

Although a hand in front of the chest would simply disappear
from the effort it takes to maintain a balance.
Though this math is secondary to his character.
Moreover, it exceeds you by the unknown: a fate

made for none. I trace down a breath
across the meadow into a group of trees
that align on both wings, an eye,

a tongue tracing
        an errant vein
that moves along your arm

leaned over your body
and let out a whisper, *I'm a stranger.*

Shining blind—by the night
—a spot of quiet in the green
that pulls a string within
            & unfurl
apply the glow from afar
to soften the edges.

Accumulate a shadow
not on the surface of the object
but within its boundaries.

The bark: phonetically ambivalent
mistakenly converted.

Monastic life
in its most primitive form
was the meaning of science.

A path itself into the mysteries of flesh
replaced beauty with a refrain from
looking at the mirror.

Today the melodic framework
is part of a name
given because of the action it performs.

In contrast, eddy motions in a rock
deepen the purposes of the map &
His Majesty's interior winds
reflect over large continents.

The many rings are an example
of limits imposed
on the growth of an old tree.

Messages travel
reshaping the scenario
they trace the surface
as the lines move in the same direction
they become less dense.

The elapsed time, an observer.
Moving horizontally in airport wind
must also rise to the weather map
belts of winds named mistakenly
there is an almost unbroken belt of ocean
that by coincidence emerged, a single reservoir.

Mechanisms of colour may sometimes reflect a stir
created by the object *changing the wind*

precisely,
marine forms in one hand   & the science of
                                                description
on the other   are a response

and landscape is a function
postulated by innumerable philosophers as
a witness in the form of changing lines, intense heat
He opined: all marine fossils, intruding magma
                    found in the folded mountains
                                             are deepening the sea
called contact.

And streams flowing over resistant rocks
form the tensile currents of
live lava valley of a thousand smokes
ash
wind
as contact between continents
creeps the other hand
like thin sheets
curve
the confluence
of short rivers with oceanic theories
& thus seaward.
Where streams meet the Master stream.

Enclaves

Exclusive to the veins that make the curl of a leaf

monsoon becomes an arrangement of planes
only his photography captures.

And as the dictionary is unable to defend its
fragmentary nature
we adjust the sun

for we are in relation to our reading
a book of themes and sensibilities
resting over the surface of a pond
an afternoon considers darker occasions

between inwardness

& intimacy

the melodic interrogation of the extreme

'pummelled on the surface of someone else's thought'

The invention of collage had a similar affect

'This blinding happiness'

A lack.

Philosophical phenomenon
as distinct movement
between two waves.

Recurring sequence
separated by its surface
from other forms
as illumination.

The presence of an arrangement
merely apparent
in faults and fractures
may exercise a repetitive way of life.

A small cage containing
the accumulation of a distant cry.

Forever Summer

Ideas flood together, boundaries break down
drawing scenarios unknown
by a coincidence

must have contemplated reality at that exact moment
a cluster of words
give it meaning by leaving it be
a condition for real experience

as the meaning of the word 'unconditional'
goes out to that unexplored world.

The question you want the audience to ask:

What does this silence do to our intimacy?
when I was the one who spoke of

this state of unknowing,
traced by infinite folds
we have a cloud of our own
spreading out on the page
as words from another language
float into our conversation

an image of your name
suspended in the helpless
distance
that began again and again
the evidence is sparse
but the answer is yes.

Fjord

lapse in the drama

a slight shift in perspective
unfolds an overall geometry

lunar prisoner,
separated forever from
event without
daylight
faces out of
a vast distance
coming ceaselessly
but never arriving

Hibiscus

flanked by

his fluid sleeve

Master

came to relax

rust

negotiating between glass & lantern

resonance of a poem

in laughter

arms of earth
falling
into the ocean
make a dangerous swell

the penguin's eggs drown

cloth dripping

a pronoun
punctuates
drying by the lamp
scar, scarf that
loved the sun
the sunny side
of a profile
against the summit
of all colours appeared
an eye (stays there,
hidden   a moment)
in mirrors collecting sunlight,
harnessing
the desert heat

An idol
    marking the arrival of summer
on a blue bodied
holdfast.

The floating world
    as a reed
        follows
    signals

not metaphor, but facts
    follow sound

Museum

Hidden things make their presence felt
in bursts of colour

painting those meanings are
a fondness for surprises

miniature in which
you guess questions
answer echoes
from the other world the other day

the wind waited on the windowsill

as a pattern beyond
edge of
consciousness
resisting a concordance
refusing to carry
what no one said

across the wings of a museum

United Pink

A small reward for remaining quiet
inarticulate yet completely intuitive
whereabouts of a building
formerly part of this planet

'I am looking over an incredible view right now.'

This distance
painted over the edge
carved into
channels that make for
strangers who feed it touches
I'm denied
to love in peace.

I heard on the news
memories mistrust muscles
as a difficulty in deciding
what regulates the rain
is now the water he drinks
drenched by the sea.

a hand held

A mute swan threatens a photographer in Tokyo
whereas the young man he loved with verses
was one amongst strangers who shared a last name
 and died the same day

❁

The light on him
a liquid
that talks back
to the arc of his lover

❁

So when the dark forces rise up to the moon
it is the moon that succumbs
to the inward smell of the exposed part
in miraculous shuffles
muscles
beat together

❁

a bud
evolved as
some sort of
the main plot

Curl

wild vine
intricate thorns
where a wing would form
slowing down in that field of snow
a trail read over hundreds of miles

❁

streams
in the gentle slope
the free flow of very minor faults.

❁

misshapen hold
on a delicate nebula

an invisible choir passing through midnight for centuries
trusted the currents of the oceans to return their men
who were off discovering new spices
                                        cheap labour
                                        exotic plants
                                        radical love
                  the unending fall
                  of sound

                  made of ash
                  your name

                  dust

                  an old friend

                  a new god

Peneplain

red earth and pouring rain
with a selection of landscapes to one side
& a tendency to praise god of his land
in various genres of song
on the other—a page, torn
between two languages is where
two tongues meet when they didn't
have characters to repeat the sound
an yes takes years to establish
hasn't had the chance to read
messages form meagre forms
a sparse world pierced in a chain
of pearls the sun sits in the middle
of the feast carving the perfect bride.

Trellis

so it is the water that carves the rocks
and wind gaps
map
migration of
warriors
fear that
messages
don't go through
someone should
fix the air.

rock flour
in a glacier
left a thick swath.

The sun seeps to the roots
the ice expands in its cracks

assigning
a depth to the atmosphere

though there is no single simple fluid to measure this response.

The prayer and the song start at the same time

We must not utter what we have found
in the shell of dust surrounding an ageing star

an unforeseen transaction with an invisible hand

relayed by constellations
(by interaction in freezing water molecules)
creates a light echo
with a cult-like new
painterly value
our want for like-mindedness.
Though later, we may store separate memories of that experience.

The silence, a cloud crossing their fate

unfolds a surprise

was some sort of god in disguise.

But,
just because the idol is made of stone
doesn't mean the devotees don't bathe it.

What we *do* is an equation

predicting our future, written in a script
that falls apart in our hands.

We are simply unable to count
what is seen as a series of shots
terrained like the sound
of laughter as the plot because
what is said would rearrange
the rest as history.

Because you must first trust
the touch for it to heal
in the eternal realm
time seen as spirit
was reduced to the silhouette
of a delicate illusion
on the various different shapes.

However, it does not follow that muscles understand
the way things move in the world.
And two objects of similar shape
manipulate the space between them, often along a path
of things moving in
a vast page are

without fixed dimensionality

a thousand avatars of the concealed
on the marble stairs
stains capture
all of consciousness.

Film

Fragments of the film survive
what she called a performance
                                                            was
      distant objects of the world put together
to bring us closer to the sounds they produce

              its shapelessness is what allowed it to grow.

The richness of a story is in the interstices precisely because
every autobiography is somewhat fictional. It echoes,
something you've never heard (of)
a film recorded over a hundred years ago.

I'm that thin ribbon of sensitive metal over a tiny slit.

Narayana has the same shirt but I don't like it.

The frames moved as if something spun out of his chest
multiple images
painted on this side of motion accrued
a hollow
regularly placed in photographs
by an early inventor of the end
believes the bright eye is a persistence

that mirrored a dream

where sound projected an interface
like an intricate arrangement of pulleys.

Blade

You said: if communication is successful the meaning will shine
through
a network of differences, but we found obscuring the basis of
language
helps manifest an intended meaning,
silence that is now an unifying impulse.

Internal structures located on the trunk of a tree
are like fur
that cover
to draw an animal
and thus simplified the hand.

Metropolis of the body
within the egg has the structure
of an eccentric mesh
that form a delicate appearance
over your palm.

Vizard

And it is by accidents received
whatever spills or ricochets
when water and fire
are one drop then another.

A forgetfulness treads
corner of eye

shape of a comma
surrounding the
irreversible silence
no font could measure

the letters can't withstand
their own agreement.

Acknowledgements

Poems from this collection have appeared in the following journals:

The Brooklyn Rail
Dusie
Recluse: St. Mark's Poetry Project
The Writer's Diner
and in several issues of *Journal 1913*

A series of poems appeared as the chapbook *Eirik's Ocean*, published by Yo-Yo Labs, Portable Press, New York, in 2016.

The author would like to thank the editors for their support.

A found-text, *The Gospels of Sri Ramakrishna and Modern Science*, served as a source of inspiration for some of the poems in this collection.

25 HarperCollins India Pvt. Ltd

Celebrating 25 Years of Great Publishing

HarperCollins India celebrates its twenty-fifth anniversary in 2017. Twenty-five years of publishing India's finest writers and some of its most memorable books – those you cannot put down; ones you want to finish reading yet don't want to end; works you can read over and over again only to fall deeper in love with.

Through the years, we have published writers from the Indian subcontinent, and across the globe, including Aravind Adiga, Kiran Nagarkar, Amitav Ghosh, Jhumpa Lahiri, Manu Joseph, Anuja Chauhan, Upamanyu Chatterjee, A.P.J. Abdul Kalam, Shekhar Gupta, M.J. Akbar, Tavleen Singh, Satyajit Ray, Gulzar, Surender Mohan Pathak and Anita Nair, amongst others, with approximately 200 new books every year and an active print and digital catalogue of more than 1,000 titles, across ten imprints. Publishing works of various genres including literary fiction, poetry, mind body spirit, commercial fiction, journalism, business, self-help, cinema, biographies – all with attention to quality, of the manuscript and the finished product – it comes as no surprise that we have won every major literary award including the Man Booker Prize, the Sahitya Akademi Award, the DSC Prize, the Hindu Literary Prize, the MAMI Award for Best Writing on Cinema, the National Award for Best Book on Cinema, the Crossword Book Award, and the Publisher of the Year, twice, at Publishing Next in Goa and, in 2016, at Tata Literature Live, Mumbai.

We credit our success to the people who make us who we are, and will be celebrating this anniversary with: our authors, retailers, partners, readers and colleagues at HarperCollins India. Over the years, a firm belief in our promise and our passion to deliver only the very best of the printed word has helped us become one of India's finest in publishing. Every day we endeavour to deliver bigger and better – for you.

Thank you for your continued support and patronage.